THE NEED TO KNOW LIBRARY™

EVERYTHING YOU NEED TO KNOW ABOUT DOMESTIC VIOLENCE

MARY P. DONAHUE, PHD

Rosen YA™
New York

This book is dedicated to the victims who face the fear, humiliation, and risk; to the survivors who keep working to effect changes in their lives; and to the thrivers—the ones who keep reaching out in the hope of finding home.

Published in 2019 by The Rosen Publishing Group, Inc.
29 East 21st Street, New York, NY 10010

First Edition

Library of Congress Cataloging-in-Publication Data

Names: Donahue, Mary P., author.
Title: Everything you need to know about domestic violence / Mary P. Donahue, Ph.D.
Description: New York : Rosen Young Adult, 2019 | Series: The need to know library | Audience: Grades 7–12. | Includes bibliographical references and index.
Identifiers: LCCN 2018006563| ISBN 9781508183464 (library bound) | ISBN 9781508183457 (pbk.)
Subjects: LCSH: Family violence—Juvenile literature. | Family violence—Prevention—Juvenile literature.
Classification: LCC HV6626 .D676 2018 | DDC 362.82/92—dc23
LC record available at https://lccn.loc.gov/2018006563

Manufactured in the United States of America

CONTENTS

INTRODUCTION

In a three-week period at the end of 2017, seventeen people died because of a bacteria outbreak in bagged lettuce. It was all over the news. Meanwhile, during any three-week period in the United States, more than sixty-three people die as a result of domestic abuse, according to the National Coalition Against Domestic Violence. That's around three per day. Most of those incidents don't make the headlines. Domestic violence is so common in our society, and all over the world, that it often goes unnoticed and unreported.

Domestic violence can be hard to recognize. Many people who are in domestic violence situations do not even realize it. Their close friends may not realize either. The key to preventing domestic violence and helping people get out of abusive situations is education. If you understand how domestic violence works, you are more likely to spot it—either in your own life or somebody else's.

The term "domestic violence" is used to describe a whole range of hostile behaviors systematically used by abusers to gain power over people and control their lives. When you hear the word "violence," you may think of physical violence—hitting, slapping, pushing, or otherwise physically harming a person—but domestic violence includes all kinds of other forms of abuse,

When someone you love hurts you, it's painful and it's wrong. But getting out of an abusive relationship is never as simple as "just leaving."

including emotional, psychological, financial, and sexual abuse. For this reason, the term "domestic abuse" is often used instead of domestic violence. Other commonly used terms are "interpersonal abuse" and "intimate partner abuse." No matter what it's called, it's all harmful and wrong, and it can have a devastating, long-term effect on the life of the person being abused.

Although the majority of domestic abuse incidents involve a male perpetrator and a female target, domestic abuse can happen to anyone in any kind of domestic relationship, including in same-sex relationships, women abusing men, parents abusing children, and adults abusing elderly relatives. Anyone can be an offender, and anyone can be a victim.

It can be upsetting to read and think about domestic violence, especially if it is something you have experienced or witnessed yourself. But when you learn to understand the patterns of abuse and how it works, you are better equipped to recognize it and work toward stopping the cycle of abuse, helping your loved ones, and helping yourself.

CHAPTER ONE

WHAT IS DOMESTIC VIOLENCE?

Domestic violence isn't one or two incidents. It is a pattern of harmful behavior made up of a whole bunch of different actions. The pattern part is what separates abuse from bad behavior. For example, a

To an outsider, it is not always obvious when a person is in an abusive relationship. Abusers usually wait until they are in a private space before becoming violent.

friend or boyfriend might be a jerk and embarrass you in public one time. This is bad behavior, for sure, but if the person is genuinely sorry and it doesn't happen again, this isn't abuse. It's a one-time incident. If it happens over and over again, that's when it becomes an abusive situation.

When people are being abused, they become fearful and uncertain. They base their sense of self on their abuser's opinion. Over time, they begin to feel invisible and their self-esteem plummets. Victims of abuse often become isolated, desperate, and dependent, and they hide it really well. You may never even suspect.

DOMESTIC VIOLENCE BY THE NUMBERS

Organizations such as the Centers for Disease Control (CDC), US Surgeon General (USSG), National Coalition Against Domestic Violence (NCADV), and various private agencies collect data that helps shed light on the epidemic of domestic violence:

In the United States, nearly twenty people per minute are physically abused by an intimate partner, according to the NCADV. In one year, this equates to more than ten million people.

Domestic abuse is the number one cause of injury to women—more than car accidents, muggings, and rapes combined, according to the USSG.

African American women experience domestic abuse at a rate 35 percent higher than that of white females and about 2.5 times the rate of women of other races, according to the US Department of Justice (USDOJ).

In a survey of Asian and Pacific Islanders, 41–60 percent of respondents reported experiencing domestic abuse, according to the Asian and Pacific Islander Institute on Domestic Violence.

Men make up approximately 15 percent of domestic abuse victims (USDOJ).

Between 40–60 percent of LGBTQ people experience domestic abuse in their lifetime (CDC).

In a domestic abuse situation, the presence of a gun increases the risk of homicide by 500 percent. Of those killed because of domestic abuse, three-fourths are female (NCADV).

Only half of domestic violence incidents are actually reported to police; only 34 percent of people who are injured by their abusers receive medical care for their injuries (NCADV).

Notice that these statistics are primarily related to physical violence. This is because physical abuse is easier to see. Other types of abuse are often done in secret and never reported, so they're impossible to measure.

THE POWER AND CONTROL WHEEL

Researchers at the Domestic Abuse Intervention Project (DAIP) in Duluth, Minnesota, interviewed thousands of women who were being abused by their partners and created a list of the most common abuse tactics used against them. The DAIP presented its findings in the shape of a wheel. The Power and Control Wheel got its name because at its very center is the goal of an

In order to stop the cycle of abuse, people need to come together and speak out publicly about their experiences of domestic violence.

abuser: power and control. From that goal come the eight categories of abusive behavior most often reported by victims.

COERCION AND THREATS

The abuser creates fear in the victim through threats like leaving her, taking the children or a pet, ruining her reputation, or threatening suicide. He may force her to do illegal things like shoplift, carry drugs, or cash bad checks. She might do these things just to stop the pain, and once she does it, the abuser has even more power.

INTIMIDATION

The abuser uses his voice, face, eyes, and body gestures to intimidate his victim in ways that other people don't see. It seems silly to tell police or a judge that "he looked at me wrong." But the victim knows what that look means, and when she sees it, she'll do whatever she can to avoid what she knows will come next. Other forms of intimidation include hurting pets, breaking property, or leaving weapons in plain sight.

EMOTIONAL ABUSE

This category includes humiliation, name-calling, rejection, blame, shouting, degrading comments, neglect, and isolation. Emotional abuse affects how you feel and what you do with those feelings; it affects how you make friends and develop your personal sense of identity.

ISOLATION

At first, protectiveness might seem sweet. It feels good when your partner wants to be with you all the time. The victim gives up friends or work gatherings to spend time with her partner. Soon, her partner begins to ask questions about where she's been, who she's been with, who she's texting, and what she's reading. He may ask for her passwords so he can monitor her social media. These tactics cut her off from her friends and family—the people who might be able to help her understand that she's in an abusive situation. The less she sees other people, the more she is forced into the reality that her abuser creates for her. She believes what he tells her.

MINIMIZING, DENYING, BLAMING

An abuser never takes responsibility for his actions. He has an excuse for everything. It's always someone else's fault. He sets up his victim to fail, then denies his involvement. For example, perhaps she needs the car to go to work. She's been late three times this month, so when her abuser leaves to go to the store, she reminds him to be home before she needs to leave. He isn't. Again. She can't get to work. Again. She's fired. He blames her, calls her names, and tells her she's useless. She tries to explain, but he twists the situation and makes her feel even worse.

Many abusers monitor their partner's email correspondence or social media engagement. They may even ask for passwords as a means of controlling a person's relationships.

USING CHILDREN

The abusive person uses the victim's children as a means of control. He may put the kids in the middle of the situation by having them relay messages. He tells her she's a bad mother and threatens to take custody of the children. He may buy them things or bribe them for information.

ECONOMIC ABUSE

The abuser controls all the finances. The victim has little to no access to money and has to account for every penny. The abuser may steal her identity and get credit cards that ruin her credit rating. He may prevent her from working and earning her own money. If she does work, she has to hand over her paycheck to him or pay for everything herself.

USING MALE PRIVILEGE

This is the social culture we live in where men are often regarded as the boss and women are expected to be submissive. Many male abusers see their authority as a right. Women have little or no ability to make their own choices. If a woman does have an opinion on something, her partner will ignore or ridicule her.

These types of abuse aren't easy to prove. That's what makes these tactics so effective. There's no real evidence.

The victim questions whether the abuse is real. If the police come to check it out, the abuser is generally good at making it look like he is in control of himself and his partner is the crazy one.

PHYSICAL AND SEXUAL ABUSE

When the nonphysical forms of abuse become boring or don't work fast enough, many abusers move on to physical and sexual abuse.

PHYSICAL ABUSE

Physical abuse is just what it sounds like. It may include punching, kicking, strangling, pinching, or biting. The abuser might use weapons like knives, lit cigarettes, boiling water, or poison. He may push his partner so she falls down the stairs, take her phone, or lock her in a room. Hurting pets and trashing property are sometimes considered forms of physical abuse.

SEXUAL ABUSE

Many abusers use sex as part of controlling a partner. The National Intimate Partner Sexual Violence Survey of 2010 found that one in six women had suffered some kind of sexual violence by a domestic abuser at some point in their lives. The abuser forces his partner to do sexual acts

Many victims of domestic abuse stay with their abusers because they fear for the safety and financial security of their children.

that she doesn't want to do, sometimes with people she doesn't want to do them with. He may wear down his victim, sometimes yelling or keeping her awake for days until she "agrees" to what he wants. Most victims don't want to talk about sexual abuse, so it's significantly underreported.

Overall, the more shame, guilt, and fear abusers can pack on, the more successful they are at controlling their partner's thoughts, feelings, and behaviors. For the victim, the psychological results can be long-lasting. She may experience problems with memory, problem solving, imagination, attention, and focusing on work. She may not trust herself enough to make decisions. Because her abuser has trained her to believe what he tells her, she may not trust what she sees herself. It is possible to undo this training and escape a domestic violence situation, but it takes patience, courage, and the right kind of support.

MYTHS AND FACTS

MYTH: I can change my abuser, if I can just....

FACT: Because survivors of domestic abuse have been trained to believe everything is their fault, they often believe they are capable of stopping the abuse if they could just find the right words or a different way to show loyalty or love. The truth is that the only person who can stop the abuse is the abuser.

MYTH: She must like it if she doesn't leave.

FACT: Victims often can't leave their abusers for many reasons, such as having no transportation or housing or being financially dependent on their abusers. They may be afraid to lose custody of their children or beloved animals. They may feel that they are better able to gauge their abuser's mood and keep themselves and their families safe when they know where he is. In fact, the most dangerous time for people in domestic violence situations is when they leave their abusers, according to the NCADV.

MYTH: The abuser just lost control for a minute. He doesn't really mean it.

FACT: Actually, abusers choose who, where, and when to hurt. The abuser hurts the person he can get away with abusing (certainly not his boss or the tough guy at the bar). He does it when he knows no one is looking or will challenge him. He doesn't break stuff that is meaningful to him. He can sense when his victim is about to give up and either leave or report him, so he changes his behavior briefly to lure her back in. Abusers are in complete control.

CHAPTER TWO

INSIDE THE MIND OF THE ABUSER

You may think you know what an abuser looks like. In reality, abusers are very good at hiding their abusive behavior. They're careful not to leave bruises where others can see. They wait to get home before they shout at their partner. They a have look or tone of voice that only their victims understand. An abuser can be anyone.

One thing that makes abusers so successful is that they're rarely all bad. Parts of them may be loveable and benevolent. They may be respected in their communities. Their children seek them out for bedtime kisses. Perhaps they coach the local soccer team or raise money for charity. They dress well. They're the life of the party. They tell funny stories. They look like everyone else.

Abusers range from the unemployed to chief executive officers. They may be community leaders, police officers and firefighters, medical personnel, teachers, social workers, or clergy members. They could be male, female, or nonbinary, gay or straight, religious or atheist, substance users, or sober. They

It's not always easy to spot an abuser. Many abusers are well-liked in their communties.

could be your friends and neighbors.

It is possible, though, to notice red flags and spot an abuser if you understand how abuse works.

RED FLAGS

Researchers have identified some common behaviors that abusers use to control their victims. Here are a few early warning signs that a relationship is becoming abusive.

QUICK INVOLVEMENT

Two people meet and start talking. They become an official couple pretty quickly. They soon move in together. The abuser uses phrases like, "When we get married" or "When we're old together," and his partner gets sucked in. It's flattering. Even if she tries to take it slowly, he puts pressure on her to move fast.

BLAMING

An abuser always seems to blame other people for things that go wrong in his life. It's a sign that he can't take personal responsibility. It's always somebody else's fault, whether it's his parents, drugs, the government, a boss, or his partner. He sees himself as the victim in his life.

POSSESSIVENESS

This is when an abuser wants to be with his partner all the time. He doesn't leave her alone. He's always

Abusers are often highly possessive. They may sulk when their partner spends time with friends or family members.

listening in on her conversations or monitoring her social media interactions. He doesn't like her best friend or her family. He doesn't want her talking to other guys. At first, it may seem sweet. In reality, he thinks he owns her.

UNREALISTIC EXPECTATIONS

In the beginning, the abuser puts his partner on a pedestal. He tells her she's perfect. The problem with that is that there's only one way off that pedestal: down. She can't meet all his expectations: She can't both work and be constantly available to him. She can't be nice to his friends and not talk to them. She can't take care of the kids and be available to go to the movies with him. He is always disappointed in her, and she feels like she's always failing.

CONSTANT MONITORING

A typical abuser checks in with his partner with nonstop texting, calling, and messaging. He tells his partner what he can and can't wear, who he can and can't hang out with, what he can and can't post on social media. He wants to know when his partner arrives someplace and when he leaves. He knows how long things should take him to do. He checks the mileage on his car. If he doesn't like something, he'll make him "pay" for it.

HYPERSENSITIVE

An abuser is easily insulted and takes everything personally. She seems to have over-the-top reactions to little frustrations and quick mood changes. It takes a lot longer to make her feel better than it took to make her mad. Her partner makes an innocent comment about the beautiful weather and suddenly

WHY DOESN'T SHE LEAVE?

When somebody you know is in an abusive relationship, you may be asking yourself why she doesn't just leave. There are lots of reasons why people don't leave abusive partners, including fear for their lives and for the lives of their children, loved ones, or pets. "The most important thing to know is that leaving is the most dangerous time for a woman," according to Anna Marjavi, program manager for Futures Without Violence. "It's the time when she's most likely to be killed." A victim may be unable to leave because she is financially dependent on her partner, or she may believe that she really loves him in spite of the abuse.

Leaving aside all the reasons why people don't leave their abusers, the question itself is flawed. It implies that the victim is responsible for making her abuser stop. A better question would be, "Why does he keep doing it?" This puts the focus on the abuser and makes him accountable for his behavior. Only the abuser can stop the abuse.

they're fighting about the mail, leaving the victim to wonder what just happened.

CYCLE OF ABUSE

If someone is being hurt by her partner, it seems logical that she would leave. It sounds simple. In reality, it's much more complicated than that. In most situations, the abuser gains power over his partner little by little. In the beginning, he may pick on her a little, but she chalks it up to his having a rough day or being hurt by a previous relationship or having poor social skills. And he says he's sorry. He wants to do better. So she begins to invest in the relationship. Over time, the abuse becomes more serious. Many abusive relationships follow a similar pattern, known as the cycle of abuse.

TEST PERIOD

The abuser throws out challenges for the victim. For example, he's really rude and hurtful one night or he makes her do something that makes her uncomfortable. He teases her. She feels silly or scared, but he convinces her to try it. Maybe it wasn't so bad, or he thanks her and promises no more uncomfortable requests. But there are more. The more she "passes" these tests, the more control he has over her.

STALKING AND ABUSE IN POP CULTURE

In popular culture, stalking behavior is often celebrated and mistaken as love. Think about the lyrics of popular songs such as "Every Breath You Take" by The Police, "Run for Your Life" by The Beatles, "One Way or Another" by Blondie, and many others. These songs celebrate stalking behavior with no regard for the needs or desires of the objects of this "love."

(continued on the next page)

If you listen closely to the lyrics of the song "Every Step You Take" by The Police, it is clearly a song about a stalker. It's important to pay attention to how relationships are depicted in pop culture.

(continued from the previous page)

In the 1998 romantic comedy *There's Something About Mary*, the main character hires a private detective to spy on his love interest and ends up winning her heart despite this creepy behavior. As Lisa Bonos writes in the *Washington Post*, "In real life, this could be the beginning of a stalking case. In 'There's Something About Mary' and other rom-coms like it, the message is: Grand gestures will make a woman fall for a man, even if she seems uninterested." In other words, he thinks he knows what she needs better than she does.

FORGIVE AND FORGET

The abuser uses the concept of "forgive and forget" —that people shouldn't hold onto past grievances—to manipulate his partner's emotions. Even if she doesn't forget, she tries to forgive him and give him another chance, waiting for things to get better.

PIECE OF CANDY

Everyone has limits. When the survivor seems like she's approaching the I've-Had-Enough stage, the abuser throws out something sweet. He buys her just the right birthday gift or they have a lovely date. Maybe they have a long talk, he cries, she forgives him, and they make up. He might even agree to seek help for anger issues. These are empty promises, but they provide hope, and maybe the abuse stops for a while.

THE EXPLOSION

The abuse begins again. The tension builds. The victim knows that something bad is coming. She waits for the screaming, swearing, name-calling, humiliation, intimidation, and/or physical abuse to happen. When it happens, it's scary and awful. The victim might start the fight herself just to get it over with. She might even end up apologizing for things that never happened. Afterward, the abuser goes from being sorry to crying to criticizing her to telling her to get over it.

After a violent episode, abusers will often express remorse and put on a show of romance in order to lure their partner back.

THE QUIET AFTER THE STORM

After the big blowup, things quiet down some. Perhaps the abuser makes an effort to come home on time or makes sure the bills are paid. The victim may laugh a little. They make holiday or birthday plans. Maybe the kids have friends over. This part gives her hope. She believes her abuser is capable of kindness, or she is capable of being a "good wife." She believes that things will be OK if she can just keep it like this.

RAMPING UP

But the tension returns. It builds. And the cycle begins all over again.

If you notice these red flags in your relationship or in the relationship of someone you know, tread carefully. It's important to understand how abuse works and the right—and wrong—ways to help yourself or a loved one get free.

CHAPTER THREE

WHAT MAKES SOMEONE A VICTIM?

Just as anyone can be an abuser, anyone can become a victim of domestic violence. Some survivors of domestic violence were abused as children and some come from stable homes. They may have one, two, or more parents, and come from working-, middle-, or upper-class households. Regardless of background, however, there are some traits common to people who become victims of domestic violence.

According to the NCADV, those things can include:

Having poor self-image or low self-esteem

Lacking emotional support and having a weak sense of identity

Being a member of a marginalized group or not speaking English (in the United States)

Confusing jealousy with love

Having an alcohol or substance abuse problem or having a partner with an alcohol or substance abuse problem

Being financially dependent on the abuser

According to the NCADV, women are particularly vulnerable to domestic abuse when they are pregnant or breastfeeding.

Having traditional beliefs about gender roles, such as that women should be submissive to men

Being pregnant or nursing

Feeling powerless in life

DEMOGRAPHICS AND CULTURAL DIFFERENCES

Domestic abuse often impacts people differently depending on who they are and their cultural backgrounds. When trying to help someone in a domestic violence situation, it's important to consider how the person's culture, sexual orientation, immigration status, and other factors affect the way she copes with the situation.

WOMEN

Until the twentieth century, women didn't have the legal right to own property, vote, keep their own wages, choose who they married, divorce their husbands, or even parent their children without male approval. There are still laws on the books in some states that declare it legal for a man to beat his wife if he only does it once a week! Such laws are no longer enforced, but they are a reminder of the injustices that women have faced and continue to face in the United States.

Women experience sexual harassment and assault at astonishingly high rates. According to RAINN, one out of six women will experience rape or attempted rape in her lifetime. Sexual violence against women is so prevalent that it is normalized in popular culture and often excused as something that boys and men can't control. In this rape culture, women who report rape and sexual assault are often blamed for what happened. People assume they must've been "asking for it" because of what they were wearing or their sexual histories. For this reason, many women don't report sexual violence to the police or even tell their friends and families. They assume that they will be blamed for it or just not believed.

Because violence against women is trivialized in these ways, women often don't realize when they are in an abusive relationship. The abuse and degradation of women is normalized in the culture and the media they see all around them.

LGBTQ COMMUNITIES

People who identify as lesbian, gay, bisexual, transgender, and queer face additional complications when

Often, same-sex couples who have children together do not have the same legal parenting rights as heterosexual couples. This can make it especially hard to leave an abusive relationship.

it comes to domestic abuse. For a start, they may not want to expose their partner's abuse for fear of giving a bad name to the broader queer community.

Moreover, many states discriminate against same-sex couples by not allowing both parents to be named as a parent on their children's birth certificates. As a result, the parent who is not on the birth certificate risks losing parental rights if the couple separates. People in this situation are far less likely to report their partner for domestic abuse.

LGBTQ people are less likely to have family support and more likely to be discriminated against by service

MUTUAL ABUSE OR SELF-DEFENSE?

Sometimes, victims of domestic abuse find themselves yelling, pushing, or otherwise lashing out at their abusers. Though it usually happens as a result of feeling overwhelmed or in danger, some people call it mutual abuse. It isn't. According to the National Domestic Violence Hotline, "Abuse is about an imbalance of power and control. In an unhealthy or abusive relationship, there may be unhealthy behaviors from both/all partners, but in an abusive relationship one person tends to have more control than the other." Often abusers will use the term "mutual abuse" to shift the blame onto their partners, but there is nothing mutual about it. As a result, the victim ends up feeling like the violence is her fault or that she deserves to be abused herself.

professionals, so it's understandable that LGBTQ victims are less likely to report abuse and seek medical treatment than their heterosexual counterparts.

COMMUNITIES OF COLOR

According to the US Department of Justice (DOJ), for women of color, "high rates of poverty, poor education, limited job resources, language barriers, and fear of deportation increase difficulty finding help and support services." In many communities of color, a strong sense of family loyalty means that the needs of an individual woman are often seen as secondary to family unity and the community at large. The DOJ reports also find that women of color are less likely to report abuse, in part because of language barriers or a lack of trust in the system. The murder rate, too, is even higher among abused women in communities of color than white women in the United States. Other cultural differences, such as religious convictions and highly regulated gender roles, may also make it harder for people of color to report abuse.

UNDOCUMENTED IMMIGRANTS

Undocumented immigrants in the United States tend to keep a low profile in order to avoid deportation. Abusers

Sometimes abusers take their victims' passports or other legal documents as a way of controlling their movements and making it harder for them to leave.

often exploit the fear of deportation by taking documents, such as passports, that could help someone obtain their legal status. They may prevent their victims from learning English or from having friends from their own culture, so that they don't have anyone to turn to for help. Many undocumented immigrants are afraid to report their abusers to authorities for fear that they will be deported and separated from their children.

YOUNG PEOPLE, DATING ABUSE, AND DIGITAL ABUSE

Domestic abuse isn't just an adult problem. Abuse of young people in relationships is often called dating abuse. A survey by the CDC shows that more than 1.5 million high school students are physically abused by their dating partners each year. Add in mental, verbal, and emotional abuse and that number is even higher. Of all those kids, only 33 percent have ever told anyone about it.

One form of abuse that is common among young people is digital abuse. This is where a person uses technology or social media to harass or intimidate a current or former romantic partner. According to Break the Cycle, digital abuse can include "demanding passwords, checking cell phones, cyberbullying, nonconsensual sexting, excessive or threatening texts, or stalking on social media."

If you or someone you know is experiencing digital abuse, tell an adult you can trust. Young abusers need to learn that their behavior is unacceptable before it becomes a habit that they carry into adulthood.

MEN

Just as women are often socialized to be affirming and gentle, men are socialized to be "tough" and to avoid expressing their feelings. They're taught to fix things and lead. So when they're being abused, it's often treated as no big deal. If a big burly guy is being abused by someone smaller than him, his experience may be viewed as nothing but a joke. Moreoever, since men are socialized not to talk about their feelings, they are less likely to seek help when they need it for fear of being seen as weak. On top of this, there are fewer community resources such as shelters or support groups for men. This leads to more isolation and more despair.

There are a few organizations that provide specific support services for men who are survivors of domestic abuse. These include Male Survivor (MaleSurvivor.org), Center Against Domestic Violence (cadvny.org), SAFE (SafeAustin.org), and the Canadian Centre for Men and Families (menandfamilies.org).

CHILDREN

In a situation where a parent is being abused, kids are often caught in the middle. They love and want to comfort the hurt parent but may not be able to because they are afraid of causing more pain, for their parent or themselves. Thus, they learn to doubt themselves. Even little kids know when something terrible is happening, but if their parent tells them everything is OK, they learn not to trust their own instincts.

Kids see much more than people think. They see the lack of respect and devaluation of the abused parent. They see the apparent strength of the abuser. And they often bring these foundational experiences into their own relationships when they grow up. In fact, a 2014 study by the National Institutes of Health shows a very strong link between witnessing domestic violence as a child and becoming a victim of domestic violence as an adult.

CHAPTER FOUR

HOW CAN I HELP?

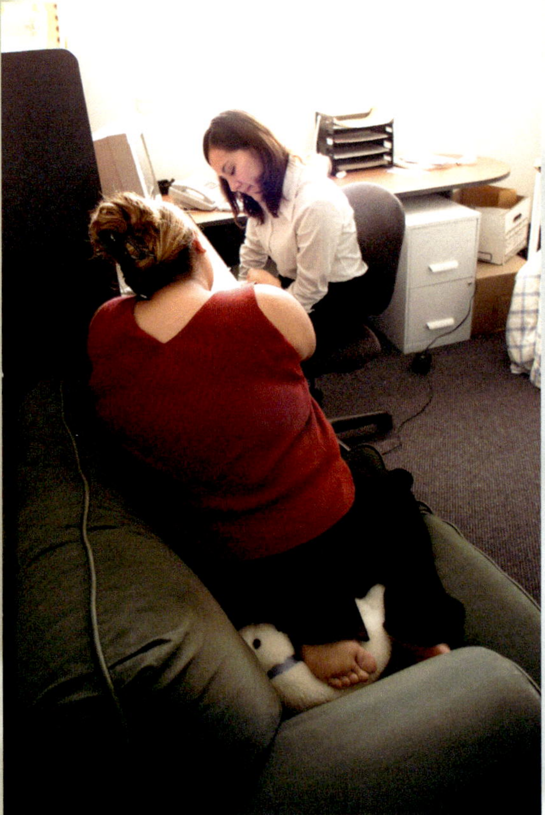

Helping a friend to leave an abusive relationship is challenging, but there are resources out there, and advocates can help.

If you have a loved one who's in a domestic violence situation, you probably want to help that person escape. This is more complicated than it seems, but it starts with approaching the person with sensitivity, good listening skills, and resources.

EXAMINE YOUR PREJUDICES

Before you can help a victim of domestic abuse, you need to examine your own assumptions about the situation. There are some commonly held but wrong ideas about domestic abuse victims:

They are stupid or weak for staying.
They can leave anytime.
They aren't protecting their children.
They are overreacting.
They just need to put their foot down.
They are mentally ill.
They like or need the abuse.

If any of these seem familiar, take some time to think more deeply about the situation.

One of the best ways to help a friend is to provide a safe, nonjudgmental space for the person to recognize her situation, feel her feelings, and figure out what comes next.

In reality, abuse survivors tend to be very resourceful. Though they are sometimes seen as passive, this is usually far from the truth. Survivors have often figured out ways to protect their children and animals from harsher abuse and delay nasty custody disputes. They have had to acquire great reserves of patience while they plan their escape. They may have learned to manage money well and construct useful safety plans. They have learned how to reach out for help without angering their abuser. They are resilient.

One of the worst things you can do is to go into this thinking you know more than the person you're trying to help.

BE PATIENT

When a survivor sees the Power and Control Wheel, she may be surprised to see that what's happening to her is called abuse. Many survivors see these behaviors as normal and believe that they themselves—not their abusers—are at fault. Survivors have learned to deny what's happening and to minimize their experiences.

To an outsider, the abuse might be evident. But the survivor has been conditioned to believe whatever her abuser says. When advocates and other helpers begin working with survivors of domestic abuse, they run into lots of strongly held notions that are simply wrong. It can be frustrating and it's important to remain patient. Even after a survivor leaves her abuser, it can take a while for her perception of the situation to change.

HELP HER HELP HERSELF

Think about why you want to help someone. You may want to just swoop in and carry the survivor away to safety, to rescue her by taking care of things. Most victims certainly need help in terms of education, resources, and emotional support. But they have to learn to do things for themselves. That's how they begin to trust themselves again. So, instead of deciding what your friend needs to do, support her in figuring it out herself. Offer your help, but let her decide when to accept it. If you try to force someone to take your help, she is likely to reject it and return to her abuser.

BELOVED BUDS

Sadly, there's a strong link between pet abuse and domestic abuse. Abusers often use pets to control their human victims. A major reason why a victim won't leave is because she fears her abuser will hurt or kill animals she loves. Try to have a plan for what to do about pets or livestock. Sometimes friends will take care of them. Some shelters allow them, but most don't. Farm animals, of course, can't go into a shelter. There are, however, some pet shelters that have fostering programs for the pets of domestic abuse victims. Also, many states allow for animals to be included in orders of protection. Be sure to ask your advocate.

LISTEN, DON'T JUST HEAR

Listening isn't the same thing as hearing. Hearing means letting someone talk while you think about what you're going to say next and how you can convince her to do what you want. Listening means really concentrating on what someone is saying. Use open body language and an open mind. Listening is about not only hearing what someone says but how she says it. Don't focus on what you think she should say. Focus on what she did say. That's her current reality, and that's what you have to work with. Offer information and resources, but don't push her to use them. Your goal isn't to make her do something. It's to illuminate the various options that are out there. The journey is hers.

SUSPEND YOUR JUDGMENT

The survivor's story might seem unbelievable. Sometimes survivors add details that didn't really happen. This may be because the person is not sure what's real and what's not or because she is testing you. She may not trust you yet. Survivors sometimes exaggerate the level of abuse because they need help and don't believe the real level of abuse is "bad enough" for someone to help. For those reasons, and many others, you must learn to listen without judgment. Her story may change a few times as she moves away from the influence of her abuser. Give her that space.

MEETING THE ABUSER

You may find yourself feeling afraid for your own well-being. The abuser might call or try to meet with you. He may threaten either directly or indirectly. He might try to give you "helpful" information about the victim and her "crazy" behavior. You should be prepared for this. You might decide to record the conversation. You might prefer to text or email, so that you have a written record. If it's necessary to meet the abuser for some reason, you should always meet in a public place, preferably with cameras around. If possible,

If you have to meet up with an abuser after leaving him, be sure to meet in a public place. Bring a friend who can keep an eye out to make sure you're safe.

bring a friend, even if he or she stays in the car. He is less likely to intimidate you if he knows there's someone watching. If the abuser steps over the line, there's a witness.

HAVE YOUR OWN SUPPORT SYSTEM

Helping someone who's in a domestic abuse situation is hard, intense, and confusing work, and you can't do it alone. You need to take care of your own physical and mental well-being, and you need to be able to reach out for help when you need it. Find a friend or therapist you can really trust to listen to you when you're feeling overwhelmed.

There are domestic abuse hotlines in every state that are open twenty-four hours a day. Advocates on those lines can give you tips, ideas, and resources. Your local police department might also have suggestions. Building a strong support system for yourself is the best way to be an effective helper.

CHAPTER FIVE

GETTING FREE

It takes a lot of courage to leave an abuser. Whether the survivor decides to leave on her own or it happens because of legal or government involvement, she will need a plan. There are many things survivors can do to make it easier to keep themselves and their loved ones safe and build a new life for themselves away from their abusers.

PREPARE A "GO BAG"

It's always a good idea for survivors to gather the things they will need before crisis hits. In building a new life, they will be asked over and over for some of the following documentation:

- Birth certificates. If the survivor is responsible for children or an elderly parent, they will need their birth certificates, too.
- Social security cards for all.
- Medications—and the prescription, if possible.

After a survivor leaves her abuser, she will need identification and other basic documentation in order to find housing, drive, or seek legal services. Keep these documents in a safe place.

- Recent photos of all, including pets.
- Ownership papers for any pet, service animal, or livestock.
- Any immigration or naturalization papers, visas, or green card paperwork.
- Marriage license and a copy of any prior divorce decrees.
- Health insurance cards or at least membership numbers and contact information.
- Credit card information and service phone numbers.
- Passports.
- Car title and insurance certificates.

- Mortgage documents.
- Income tax reports.
- School and vaccine records.
- A list of important phone numbers. Even if they're saved on a phone or computer, it's a good idea to have them in writing. Technology has a way of disappearing sometimes.

Gather originals of these documents (or at least a good copy) and keep them in a safe place. These could be kept at a friend's house or mailed to a trusted person.

A go bag should include an untraceable cell phone and some clothing. Many victims find themselves fleeing the house with no way to get back right away. If you have clothes, money, and paperwork stored somewhere away from home, you can have access to it immediately.

MONEY

Survivors may need to save money before they can leave. This is hard if they are financially dependent on their abuser. They should try to save money a little at a time in ways that the abuser won't notice. Find a place to hide cash that is unlikely to be discovered, perhaps even at a trusted friend's house. In addition to cash, they might think about opening a bank account without the abuser's knowledge. They could have the bank statements sent to a friend's house. It's helpful to have a place for loans or paychecks to be deposited. Think about gathering up any jewelry or other valuables that could be sold if necessary.

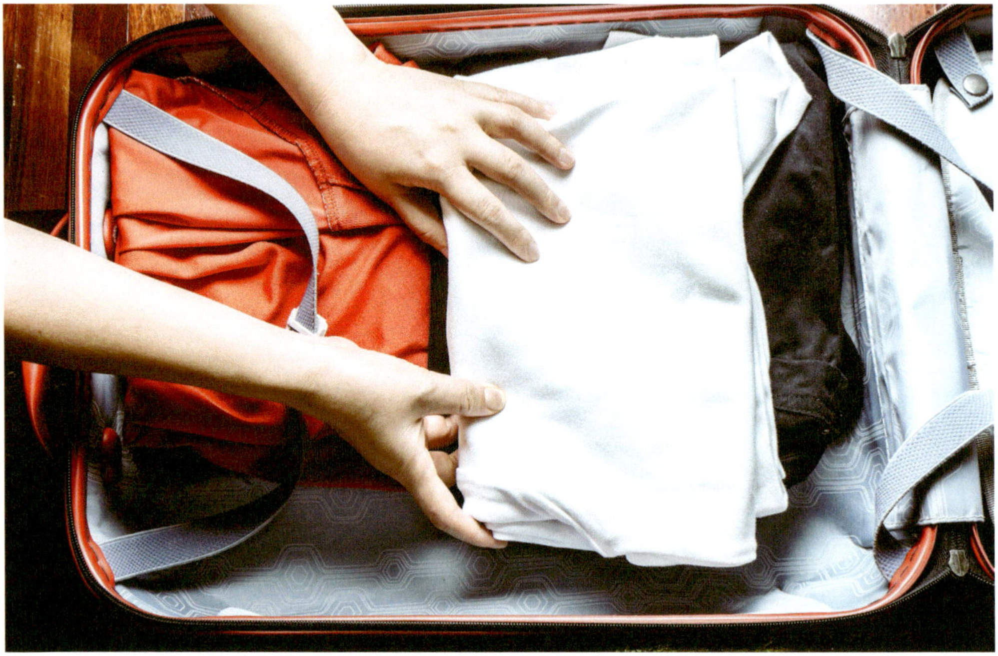

A person may have to flee a domestic violence situation in a hurry. It's a good idea to pack a bag of essentials ahead of time.

FINDING ADVOCACY

Getting out of an abusive situation is much easier if a person has help. When someone is being abused, it's hard to think clearly. The abuser may have cut the survivor off from friends and family. It's helpful to find someone who's trained in the area of domestic abuse, who can ask the right questions and reflect accurately. This is where domestic abuse organizations come in.

A good first step is to call the National Domestic Violence Hotline at 1-800-787-7233. This organization can connect survivors with their local service providers and shelters. They may have to make a few phone calls to find the closest advocates.

Local advocates will be able to give the best information regarding state and local laws, resource locations, custody questions, and other everyday concerns. Try to think of specific questions to ask. Take notes. Advocates will ask questions about the situation to figure out how best to advise the survivor. Note that survivors may have to tell their story more than once. Different types of advocates will be looking for different information. If the survivor is not comfortable with an advocate for some reason, he or she can request a different person.

ORDER OF PROTECTION?

A survivor may decide to get an order of protection to keep her abuser away. If the police arrest him, there may be bail conditions that tell him to keep away. A victim may also request a formal order of protection herself. Talk to an advocate or a lawyer about this; experts in domestic abuse issues will know what to ask and listen for what is needed. These people might also help the survivor to decide whether the order is a good idea. In some cases, an order might make the violence more intense. It is essentially just a piece of paper and the abuser may ignore it. On the other hand, an order can help police and other outsiders recognize the seriousness of the situation. Some abusers are more likely to listen to a judge and the threat of jail than to a pastor, friend, or lawyer.

CHILDREN

If the survivor shares children or property with the abuser, there are many legal steps to take once she leaves. It's not a good idea to make major decisions or sign anything without professional advice. Many survivors have trouble thinking clearly, and sometimes people end up giving up their children, homes, or financial assets just to make an abuser go away. Chances are, he's not going away, and they can't get back what they've given away.

Testifying against an abuser in court can be emotionally exhausting and traumatizing. Be sure to bring family members or friends along for support.

TECHNOLOGY

Technology is changing all the time. It's easy to place a camera or tracking device in a house, purse, car, or computer. If you've ever wondered how an abuser could possibly know something you thought you'd kept hidden, it's possible he has some form of tracking. For example, there are computer programs that track keystrokes and save deleted information. In making a getaway plan, try to use a library computer or a friend's computer.

Sometimes survivors of domestic violence have to leave behind a beloved pet when they leave their partner. Saying good-bye to a pet can be devastating.

The same goes for phones. Someone may be recording your calls without your knowledge. Also, because cell phones work wirelessly, there are devices that can listen in to calls while someone sits in a car. Conversations can be monitored even if a phone or computer is turned off. Even if you delete your text messages, there may still be ways for an abuser to get them.

CODE WORD

Once an abuser knows he has lost control of his victim, he is more likely to be violent. Whether or not the survivor is still with her abuser, she should think of a code word that she can use to signal to others that she needs immediate help or to be prepared for a violent outburst. It should be a fairly common word or phrase that the survivor and her supporters can easily remember but that won't alert the abuser.

COMMUNICATING WITH THE ABUSER

After the survivor leaves, she may have to keep in touch with her abuser if she lives in a small town or they have children together. It's important to have a plan for how to communicate with the abuser. Hearing his voice may send the survivor right back in time, so many advocates suggest relaying messages by email or text rather than talking on the phone. Talking also provides a chance for the abuser to harass the survivor or try to convince her to come back. Emailing or texting allows the survivor to take time to form a response.

If the survivor has to talk to her abuser, she should plan ahead of time what she needs to say and stick to it. Don't engage in any other conversation or get defensive. Try not to become angry or apologize. Just focus on delivering the message, whether or not the abuser is listening.

FIND A THERAPIST

Being in an abusive relationship has a long-lasting impact on a person's mental health. Even after a survivor leaves, she may find that she is forgetful, numb, or disorganized. Maybe she sleeps too much or has terrible nightmares. She might go from being super angry to sobbing uncontrollably. In the beginning, she might even think things were easier when she was with her abuser, when she didn't have to think about what to do next—she just did what he said. Making decisions and fearing mistakes can be crushing.

It's a good idea for survivors to find a mental health therapist who is trained in domestic abuse issues to help them process their emotions. Find someone with professional training and experience, because people without training are unlikely to understand the nuances of how domestic abuse works.

THE EQUALITY WHEEL

When a person is in a domestic abuse situation, it may be hard to imagine life on the other side. But many survivors find happy, fulfilling, and equitable relationships after they escape their abusive relationships. It may help to check out the Equality Wheel. Like the Power and Control Wheel, the Equality Wheel was created by DAIP, home of the Duluth Model, and it can be found at theduluthmodel.org.

At the center of this wheel is equality, which is at the center of all healthy relationships. It consists of things like negotiation and fairness, respect, trust and support, honesty, and accountability. It reminds people of the importance of things like feelings and opinions, reliability, and the financial and sexual responsibility of both parties. Keeping those things in mind, there is no room for violence. Try keeping a picture of the Equality Wheel on your desk to remind you to live by those rules every day.

People in abusive relationships often feel that there's no hope for change, but by facing their fear, planning carefully, and getting the right help, victims can move from survivors to thrivers and role models.

10 QUESTIONS TO ASK A DOMESTIC VIOLENCE ADVOCATE

1. How can I help my friend without putting her and myself in danger?
2. My friend doesn't believe that her partner is being abusive. How can I persuade her to leave him?
3. When someone hurts me, how do I know if it's really abuse?
4. I want to leave my partner, but I'm afraid it will make things worse. What can I do to keep myself and my family/pets safe?
5. My abuser isolated me from my friends and family, and now I don't have anyone to talk to. Where can I go for support?
6. I'm afraid my abuser is stalking me and tracking my phone/social media. What can I do?
7. Should I file an order of protection? How will it help me?
8. I've had three abusive partners. What can I do to make sure my next partner doesn't abuse me?
9. How can I find a therapist who specializes in domestic abuse?
10. How can I find a support group for survivors of domestic abuse?

GLOSSARY

abuser Someone who uses violence or cruelty to control another person or an animal, especially on a regular basis.

advocate A person who works to support and speak up for another person or group of people.

code word A previously agreed on word that alerts the listener to take action.

coerce To use threats or fear to force someone to do something he or she doesn't want to do.

digital abuse The use of technology and social media to intimidate, harass, or threaten someone. This includes cyberbullying, nonconsensual sexting, and stalking on social media.

domestic abuse A pattern of cruel behavior used by one partner against the other, with the intention of gaining power and control over that person. This can include physical, emotional, financial, psychological, digital, or sexual abuse.

emotional abuse Name-calling, insults, mocking, yelling, and humiliation used to invoke guilt and shame in the victim.

equality wheel A visual aid designed to help people identify important aspects of an intimate relationship.

financial abuse Using money and credit as a means of controlling the victim.

go bag A bag packed ahead of time and stored in a safe location that contains important items the survivor will need in order to gain independence after leaving an abuser.

orders of protection A court order that makes it illegal for an abuser to contact or be near the victim, except for in specific ways that may be written in the order.

pet abuse Cruelty toward animals, including hitting, kicking, yelling at, or neglecting to feed the animal. Abusers often use pet abuse to control people.

physical abuse The use of physical force to harm another person. Includes slapping, pushing, hitting, shutting someone in a room, and property destruction.

power and control wheel A visual aid designed to illustrate common tactics used by domestic abusers to control their victims.

psychological abuse The use of psychological means to harm someone. Includes ignoring or isolating someone, hiding things that someone needs, controlling someone's movements, and deliberately giving someone inaccurate information that harms them.

red flag Common signs and behaviors that may indicate that a relationship is abusive.

self-esteem A person's sense of her own value; the amount of confidence she has in her own abilities and knowledge.

sexual abuse Forcing or coercing a person to engage in sexual acts against his or her will.

survivor (of domestic violence) A person who has been a victim of domestic violence and is working to leave or has already left her abuser.

victim (of domestic violence) A person who is being abused by an intimate partner.

FOR MORE INFORMATION

Canadian Centre for Men and Families
201-2 Homewood Avenue
Toronto, ON M4Y2J9
Canada
(647) 479-9611 or toll free at (1-844) 900-2263
Website: http://www.menandfamilies.org
Facebook, Instagram, and Twitter: @ menandfamilies
This organization provides mentoring and support for male victims of abuse and violence, including therapy, peer support, and a legal clinic.

Centers for Disease Control and Prevention
1600 Clifton Road
Atlanta, GA 30329
(800) 232-4636, (888) 232-6348
Website: https://www.cdc.gov
Facebook: @CDC
Instagram and Twitter: @CDCgov
This US government agency is dedicated to tracking and improving overall health. The section on violence prevention on the website provides information and resources regarding many forms of domestic abuse.

Domestic Abuse Intervention Project (DAIP)
202 East Superior Street
Duluth, MN 55802
(218) 722-2781
Website: https://www.theduluthmodel.org

The home of the Duluth Model and the creator of the Power and Control Wheel, this organization works to end violence against women via local programs and partnerships with other domestic violence organizations around the world.

Ending Violence Association of Canada
1404-510 West Hastings Street
Vancouver, BC V6B 1L8
Canada
(604) 633-2506
Website: http://endingviolencecanada.org
This Canadian national nonprofit organization works to eliminate gender-based violence, including sexual violence, intimate partner violence, and child abuse, by providing education, programs, and resources.

National Domestic Violence Hotline
PO Box 161810
Austin, TX 78716
(512) 453-8117, Hotline: (1-800) 799-7233
Website: http://www.thehotline.org
Facebook: @nationaldomesticviolencehotline
Instagram: @ndvhofficial
Pinterest: @ndvhotline
Twitter: @ndvh
This national hotline provides information for survivors and friends of survivors seeking information and resources regarding domestic abuse. The organization can provide callers with contact information for local organizations and advocates.

National Institute of Mental Health
Office of Science Policy, Planning, and Communications
Science Writing, Press, and Dissemination Branch
6001 Executive Boulevard
Room 6200, MSC 9663
Bethesda, MD 20892
(301) 443-4513, (1-866) 615-6464 (toll free)
TTY: (301) 443-8431, (1-866) 415-8051 (toll free)
Website: http://www.nimh.nih.gov
Facebook: @NIMH.NIH.GOV
Twitter: @NIMH.NIH.GOV
This federal agency of the US government leads research on mental disorders. The website provides comprehensive information and resources regarding mental health.

National Resource Center on Domestic Violence
6041 Linglestown Road
Harrisburg, PA 17112
(800) 537-2238
Website: www.nrcdv.org
Facebook: @NRCDV
Twitter: @NRCDV
Tumblr: nationaldvam.tumblr.com
This national organization provides comprehensive information, training, and services with the goal of improving community response to domestic violence.

FOR FURTHER READING

Bancroft, Lundy. *Why Does He Do That? Encouragement for Women Involved with Angry and Controlling Men.* New York, NY: Penguin Publishing Group, 2015.

Bancroft, Lundy, and J. A. C. Patrissi. *Should I Stay or Should I Go? A Guide to Knowing if Your Relationship Can—Or Should—Be Saved.* New York, NY: Berkley Books, 2011.

Bancroft, Lundy, J. G. Silverman, and Daniel Ritchie. *The Batterer as Parent: Addressing the Impact of Domestic Violence on Family Dynamics.* Los Angeles, CA: SAGE, 2012.

Banks, Delilah, and John Giacobello. *Surviving Family Violence.* New York, NY: Rosen Publishing, 2016.

Baruch-Felman, Caren, and Thomas R. Hoerr. *The Grit Guide for Teens: A Workbook to Help You Build Perseverance, Self-Control, and a Growth Mindset.* Oakland, CA: Instant Help Books, 2017.

Dominy, Amy Fellner. *Die for You.* New York, NY: Delacorte Press, 2016.

Eastham, Chad. *The Truth About Dating, Love, and Just Being Friends.* Nashville, TN: Thomas Nelson, 2011.

Ginsburg, Kenneth R., and Martha M. Jablow. *Building Resilience in Children and Teens: Giving Kids Roots and Wings.* American Academy of Pediatrics, 2015.

Lowery, Zoe. *Gender-Based Violence and Women's Rights.* New York, NY: Rosen Publishing, 2018.

Parker, S. M. *The Girl Who Fell.* New York, NY: Simon Pulse. 2016

BIBLIOGRAPHY

Bancroft, Lundy. *How to Spot Red Flags When Dating.* Audacious Life Podcast, July 15, 2017. https://www.youtube.com/watch?v=gYw56aerD0U.

Bonos, Lisa. "In Romantic Comedies, It's Cute. In Real Life, It's Stalking." *Washington Post*, February 26, 2016. https://www.washingtonpost.com/news/soloish/wp/2016/02/26/in-romantic-comedies-its-romantic-in-real-life-its-stalking/?utm_term=.56a78c374b86.

Break the Cycle. "Learn About Dating Abuse." Retrieved February 27, 2018. https://www.breakthecycle.org/learn-about-dating-abuse.

Evans, Patricia. *The Verbally Abusive Relationship: How to Recognize It and How to Respond.* Avon, MA: Adams Media, 2010.

Martin, Sandra L., Jennet Arcara, and McLean D. Pollock. "Violence During Pregnancy and the Postpartum Period." VAWnet, December 2012. https://vawnet.org/material/violence-during-pregnancy-and-postpartum-period.

National Center for Domestic and Sexual Violence. "Power and Control Wheel." Retrieved February 15, 2018. http://www.ncdsv.org/images/PowerControlwheelNOSHADING.pdf.

National Domestic Violence Hotline. "Get the Facts and Figures." Retrieved January 30, 2018. http://www.thehotline.org/resources/statistics.

National Domestic Violence Hotline. "The Myth of Mutual Abuse," January 25, 2016. http://www

.thehotline.org/2016/01/25/myth-of-mutual-abuse.

NiCarthy, Ginny. *Getting Free: A Handbook for Women in Abusive Relationships.* Berkeley, CA: Seal Press, 1982.

Overwhelmed Brain. "Why Do Abusers Abuse?" October 14, 2017. https://www.youtube.com/watch?v=-2HMn5WBrwA.

Tsavoussis, Areti. "Child-Witnessed Domestic Violence and Its Adverse Effects on Brain Development: A Call for Societal Self-Examination and Awareness." Frontiers in Public Health, October 10, 2014. https://www.ncbi.nlm.nih.gov/pmc/articles/PMC4193214.

Violence Policy Center. "When Men Murder Women: An Analysis of 2015 Homicide Data." September 2017. http://www.vpc.org/studies/wmmw2017.pdf.

Walters, M. L., J. Chen, and M. J. Breiding. *The National Intimate Partner and Sexual Violence Survey (NISVS): 2010 Findings on Victimization by Sexual Orientation.* Atlanta, GA: National Center for Injury Prevention and Control, 2013.

Widom, Cathy Spatz, Sally Czaja, and Mary Ann Dutton. "Child Abuse and Neglect and Intimate Partner Violence Victimization and Perpetration: A Prospective Investigation." *Child Abuse and Neglect:* 38(4), pp. 650–663. April 2014.

Women of Color Network Facts and Stats. "Domestic Violence in Communities of Color," June 2006. http://www.doj.state.or.us/wp-content/uploads/2017/08/women_of_color_network_facts_domestic_violence_2006.pdf.

INDEX

ABOUT THE AUTHOR

Mary P. Donahue earned her doctoral degree in counseling psychology from the University at Albany, State University of New York. She maintains a clinical practice specializing in grief and trauma with both adolescents and adults. Dr. Donahue works extensively with people whose lives are impacted by domestic and dating abuse, in both clinical and forensic settings. She and her family work and play worldwide while living happily in southern Maine.

PHOTO CREDITS

Cover OndroM/Shutterstock.com; p. 5 Odua Images/Shutterstock.com; p. 7 Dragon Images/Shutterstock.com; pp. 7, 17, 27, 36, 43 (background) Sdecoret/Shutterstock.com; p. 10 John Gomez/Shutterstock.com; p. 12 Wayhome Studio/Shutterstock.com; p. 15 Tanya Constantine/Blend Images/Getty Images; p. 18 Brand X Pictures/Stockbyte/Thinkstock; p. 19 JackF/iStock/Thinkstock; p. 23 Koh Hasebe/Shinko Music/Getty Images; p. 25 Stockfour/Shutterstock.com; p. 28 Monkey Business Images/Shutterstock.com; p. 30 Monkey Business Images/iStock/Thinkstock; p. 32 Shahfarshid/iStock/Thinkstock; p. 36 Bob Carey/Los Angeles Times/Getty Images; p. 37 wavebreakmedia/Shutterstock.com; p. 41 AshTproductions/Shutterstock.com; p. 44 M. Unal Ozmen/Shutterstock.com; p. 46 Art_Photo/Shutterstock.com; p. 48 RichLegg/E+/Getty Images; p. 49 Daxiao Productions/Shutterstock.com.

Design: Michael Moy; Layout: Ellina Litmanovich;
Editor: Rachel Aimee; Photo Researcher: Sherri Jackson